Core Knowledge Language Arts®

The Age of Exploration
Unit 9 Reader
Skills Strand
GRADE 3

Amplify learning.

Core Knowledge®

Table of Contents
The Age of Exploration
Unit 9 Reader

Introduction to *The Age of Exploration* 2

Chapter 1: The Lure of Spices 6

Chapter 2: Second Sons 14

Chapter 3: Toscanelli's Map 22

Chapter 4: Navigation in the Age of Exploration 30

Chapter 5: El Castillo de San Marcos 40

Chapter 6: Coronado Reports to the King 48

Chapter 7: John Cabot 58

Chapter 8: Henry Hudson 70

Chapter 9: The Fur Trade and Samuel de Champlain 76

Chapter 10: A History of People in North America 88

Chapter 11: Caribbean Words 98

Glossary for *The Age of Exploration* 111

Introduction to
The Age of Exploration

In 1491, most Europeans did not know that North and South America existed. The people of the Americas did not know that Europe existed. Although other **explorers** had visited the Americas before, Europeans did not know that.

In 1492, that changed. In that year, Christopher Columbus sailed across the Atlantic Ocean and accidentally landed on islands off the coast of the Americas. His **explorations** marked the start of the Age of **Exploration**.

An artist's illustration of Columbus landing in the New World

As news spread about what Columbus had found, men from all over Spain raced to find treasure. Spanish **conquistadors**, such as Francisco Vasquez de Coronado, set out in search of silver and gold. They **slashed** their way through swamps. They marched across deserts. They **explored** and conquered many lands.

A few years later, other European countries got involved. John Cabot went **exploring** for England. Henry Hudson **explored** for England and for the Netherlands. Samuel de Champlain **explored** for France.

These **explorers** changed the world. They connected Europe with the Americas. You will read about some of their journeys here.

Some European Explorers

Explorers	Name	Source of Funding
	Christopher Columbus	Spain
	Francisco Vasquez de Coronado	Spain
	John Cabot	England
	Henry Hudson	England Dutch East India Company (Netherlands)
	Samuel de Champlain	France

The Lure of Spices

Chapter 1

Many European explorers were hoping to find gold and other **precious** metals.

You can probably understand why explorers were eager to find gold. Gold is a valuable metal even today. However, you may be surprised to learn that many explorers were also excited about finding **spices**. You might be saying, "**Spices**? Really? Why were they so eager to find **spices**?"

Here's the answer: Things that are **scarce**, or hard to find, tend to be **expensive**. That's why gold is **expensive** today. That's also why **spices** were **expensive** five hundred years ago. Back then, **spices** were **scarce** in Europe. They were hard to find. So they cost a lot. Some **spices** were almost worth their weight in gold.

Gold

The red balls in the center of this image are red **peppercorns**. A cook can add a few whole **peppercorns** to soup. He can use a spice grinder to **grind** the **peppercorns** into tiny bits. Either way, the pepper will add **flavor** to the soup. It will make the soup spicier and tastier.

To the left of the red **peppercorns**, you can see white **peppercorns**. These come from the same plants as red **peppercorns** but they are prepared in a different way. White **peppercorns** start out as red **peppercorns** but the outer **hull** of the red **peppercorn** is removed to reveal the inner **kernel**, which is white. They can be used in the same way as red **peppercorns**.

The black bowl in the upper right of this image is filled with cloves. Cloves are dried flower buds. They are used to add **flavor** to meats and stews, some teas, and pumpkin pie. Cloves are very strong. Cooks who use them must be careful because adding too many of them may **overwhelm** other **flavors** in the dish.

Spices displayed in a *spice* market

Peppercorns can't be grown in Europe. They can only be grown in warm, wet places, like India. The image shows unharvested **peppercorns**.

Today, we can get **peppercorns** from India pretty easily. An airplane or a ship can transport large amounts of them. You can go to a grocery store and get almost any **spice** you want. A little jar of cloves might cost a dollar or two. A can of **peppercorns** might cost five or six dollars.

Five hundred years ago, Europeans were not so lucky. The world was not as well connected as it is today. **Spices** were hard to get and transport. They cost a lot of money.

A Spaniard who wanted pepper would have to pay for a lot more than just the pepper. He would have to pay the cost of shipping the pepper over land all the way from India, using donkeys, mules, and camels.

Unharvested **peppercorns**

It was the same with cloves and cinnamon. These plants could not be grown in Europe. They had to be **imported**, or brought in, to Europe from faraway places, like the Indies.

Many of the **spices** we use are the flowers, the fruits, or the seeds of the plant. Cinnamon is different. In this case, the part of the plant we use is the bark. Strips of bark are cut off the tree. The outer bark is cut away. The inner bark is kept and rolled up like little **scrolls**. These are called cinnamon sticks. Cinnamon can also be **ground** up, like pepper.

Do you like the taste of cinnamon? Do you like cinnamon on toast? How much do you like it? Would you be willing to sail across an ocean to get some cinnamon for your toast? In a sense, that is what European explorers were trying to do.

Star anise, cinnamon, and cloves (clockwise from star anise)

2 Second Sons

Did you know that many explorers had older brothers? Very few of them were the oldest sons in their families.

Can you guess why that might be?

It's not because firstborn children didn't want to go out and explore the world. It has to do with the laws in Europe at the time. Most countries in Europe had laws about who could **inherit** an **estate**. These laws stated that the oldest son in a family would **inherit** all of his father's land, goods, and money.

This was true for kings. When a king died, he would be replaced on the **throne** by his eldest son. A daughter could only become queen if a king had no sons.

Charles V (an oldest son) became King of Spain after his father died.

This was also true for **nobles**. For example, if the Duke of Richland died, his eldest son would become the new Duke of Richland. This eldest son would **inherit** everything his father owned.

What did the younger sons and daughters get? Nothing.

This system is known as primogeniture. Primo means "first." "Geniture" means born. Primogeniture is a system in which the firstborn son **inherits** everything when his father dies.

This way of doing things seems very strange to us today. It also seems unfair. Most parents today would not leave all their money and **property** to their oldest son. They would split the money and **property** up among all their children. Why, then, did Europeans do things differently back in the 1400s and 1500s?

*According to the system of primogeniture, the oldest son, Son 1, would **inherit** everything his father owned.*

There is actually a good reason. Let's go back to the Duke of Richland. Imagine that he is a wealthy landowner living in a land with no law of primogeniture. Let's say he owns 1,000 acres of good farmland. But, alas, he dies. His land is split between his two sons. So now we have two men, each of whom has 500 acres of land. Now, suppose each of these two men has four sons. When the fathers die, their lands are split again. So now we have eight men with 125 acres each. Do you see what is happening? The **estate** of Richland is being split up. It is no longer big and **impressive**. It is becoming small and unimportant. The men of Richland are probably also becoming less powerful because they each have less land.

Also, who is the Duke of Richland now? Are all eight of his grandsons now dukes? Will their grandsons also be dukes? At this rate, the land will be **overrun** by dukes!

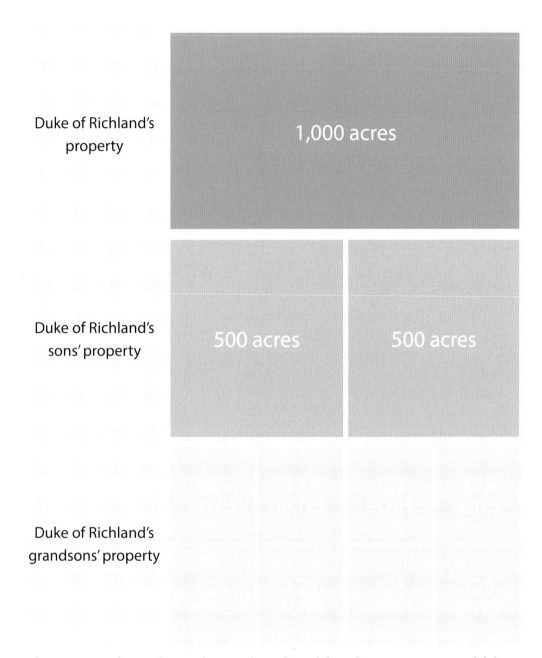

Duke of Richland's property — 1,000 acres

Duke of Richland's sons' property — 500 acres, 500 acres

Duke of Richland's grandsons' property

This image shows how the Duke of Richland's property would be split.

The **nobles** did not want this to happen. They wanted to keep their lands together, so their families would remain powerful. They wanted there to be one Duke of Richland and they wanted him to remain one of the most powerful men in the country. That is why they passed laws of primogeniture.

This was good news for the oldest son in each family. It was bad news for the other sons and for all the daughters. They had to find other ways to make money and gain power.

One way to do this was to be an explorer. If you could not **inherit** anything in your homeland, why not sail off and discover some other way to make your fortune?

This is, in fact, what many second sons did in the late 1400s and 1500s. They went in search of ways to make money they would never have **inherited** if they stayed in Europe.

Many second sons sailed off to find their own riches.

3 Toscanelli's Map

An Italian man named Paolo [POW-loe] Toscanelli [TOS-kəh-NEL-ee] may have been responsible for the Europeans landing in the Americas.

Toscanelli was a math **whiz**, an astronomer, and a mapmaker. In 1474, he made a map of the world, which he sent with a letter to the King of Portugal telling how to reach the Indies by sailing west. The King was very interested but Toscanelli was not correct.

On the right side of Toscanelli's map, you can see some parts of Europe in orange. You may know some of them: Ireland, labeled "Irlanda;" London, England; and Lisbon, Portugal, labeled "Lisbona."

To the south of Europe, you can see part of Africa. The part Europeans called Guinea is labeled. The Canary Islands, just off the coast of Africa, are labeled "Canariae."

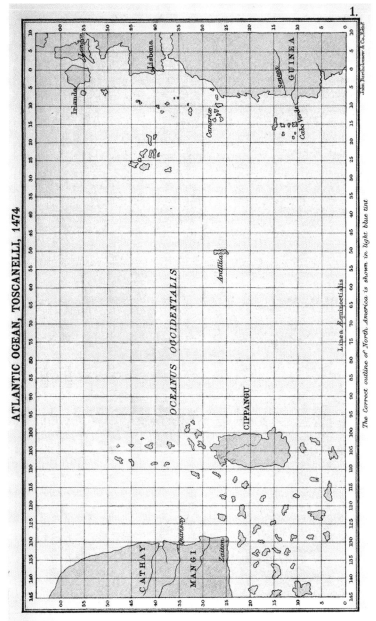

ATLANTIC OCEAN, TOSCANELLI, 1474

The right side of this map is mostly correct.

The Correct outline of North America is shown in light blue tint.

Look at the left side of the map. This side shows parts of Asia, or, rather, it shows parts of Asia where Toscanelli thought they might be.

Do you see the big island labeled Cippangu? That was what Toscanelli and other Europeans called Japan. They had heard about Japan. They knew it was somewhere in Asia. But they did not know exactly where. Toscanelli put it on his map where he thought it might be.

Do you see the land labeled Cathay Mangi? That was what Toscanelli and others of his day called China. They had read about China in a book called *The Travels of Marco Polo*. But they did not know exactly where it was. Again, the map shows where Toscanelli thought China was, not where it really is.

Do you see the islands just south of Cathay Mangi? Those are parts of the Indies. They are the "spice islands" that Europeans were so eager to reach.

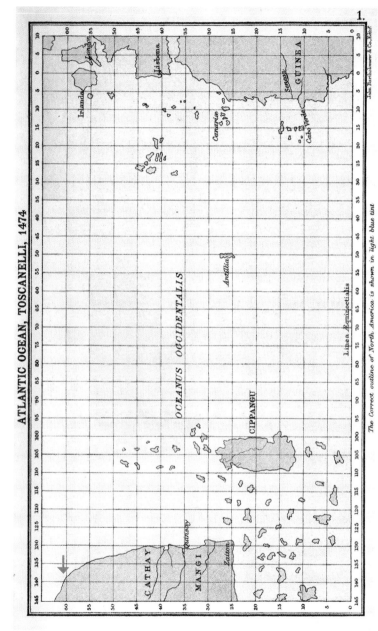

ATLANTIC OCEAN, TOSCANELLI, 1474

The Correct outline of North America is shown in light blue tint

The left side of the map is what Toscanelli thought was there.

Notice that Asia does not seem to be too far from Europe. That was one of Toscanelli's big ideas. He thought Earth was not that big. He thought Asia was probably not too far from Europe. So that's how he drew it on his map.

Now, imagine you are Christopher Columbus. You want to find a way to get to the Indies. You look at Toscanelli's map.

"Wow!" you say. "Look at that! Asia is right there. It's not so far from Europe. There's nothing in between but a little water! It would not be hard to get to Asia! Why, I could get there in a few weeks. All I would need to do is sail west!"

We can never be sure what was in Christopher Columbus's mind when he first looked at Toscanelli's map. We do know he made a plan to travel to the Indies based on Toscanelli's map. Then, he set out to find someone who would pay for his **voyage**. In the end, he **convinced** King Ferdinand and Queen Isabella of Spain to pay for it.

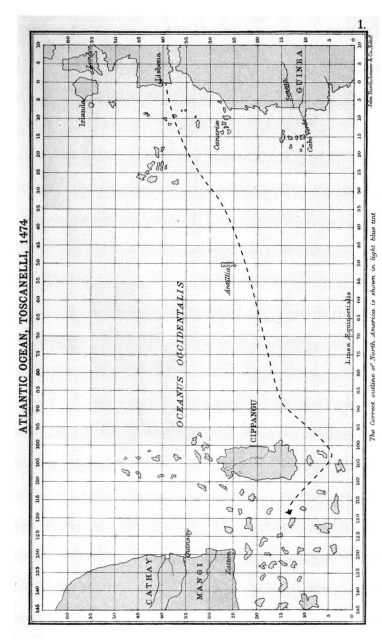

The route Columbus planned to take

Now, here is the same map with something added. The light blue shows what is really there, not what Toscanelli thought was there. You can see the outline of North America and part of South America.

The orange parts of the map show the Asian lands Columbus **expected** to reach. The light blue outline shows the lands where he actually accidentally landed.

Toscanelli's map explains a lot. It helps us see where Columbus got the idea of sailing west to reach the Indies. It also helps us see why he ran into the islands of the Caribbean and why he thought he was close to China.

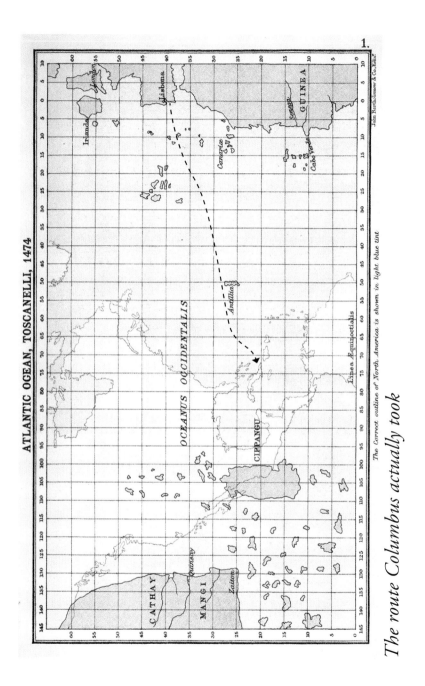

ATLANTIC OCEAN, TOSCANELLI, 1474

The Correct outline of North America is shown in light blue tint

The route Columbus actually took

Navigation in the Age of Exploration

Do you ever go on trips with your family? How do the adults in your family find the places they want to visit? Do they write down directions? Do they use maps? Do they look for **landmarks** along the way? Do they have an electronic **device** that tells them where to turn?

Early European explorers didn't have most of those things. Most sailors in those days stayed close to land and looked for familiar **landmarks**. However, this would not work for explorers. They could not look for familiar **landmarks** because they were sailing into unknown waters.

Early explorers did have some maps but they were not always **accurate**. So how did the explorers **keep track** of where they were?

Things we use today to find places we want to visit

They had several tools that they might have used. One of them was a **compass**. A **compass** is a very simple **device**. It is just a little **magnet** that sits on a pin so it can spin. The pointer on the **magnet** points north. Back then, nobody knew why. Now, we know it's because Earth has a **magnetic field**, which is strongest at the poles. **Magnets** are attracted to the **magnetic field** of the North Pole.

Using a **compass**, a sailor could figure out which direction was north. Plus, if he knew which direction was north, he could figure out south, east, and west. That was a big help.

*A **compass***

Explorers also used the stars to **keep track** of their position. Sailors in this day used two **gadgets**. One was called a quadrant. The other one was called an astrolabe. The details of how these **gadgets** work are complicated but the basic idea is not. The idea is that you can **keep track** of your position on Earth by **keeping track** of where certain stars appear to be in the night sky. If you can tell where the sun, the North Star and other key stars are, you should be able to figure out where you are on Earth.

An astrolabe (top) and quadrant

Others may have **kept track** of how far they had traveled using a **method** called **dead reckoning**.

Here's how **dead reckoning** worked: a sailor had a piece of wood that was tied to a rope. The rope was knotted at regular intervals. There might be a knot every five feet. The sailor would toss the piece of wood overboard while the ship was sailing. When the wood hit the water, the sailor would turn over an **hourglass**.

The sailor or the captain of the ship would then watch to see how much rope was pulled out of the ship and into the sea. If the ship was going fast, it would quickly leave the piece of wood behind. It would pull many yards of rope out of the ship before the **hourglass** ran out. If the ship was going slower, it would not pull as much rope out. Then, the person would count how many knots of rope got pulled out of the ship before the **hourglass** emptied out. If you have ever heard of a ship's speed referred to as knots, this is a **forerunner** of that measurement of speed.

Dead reckoning *helped sailors* ***keep track*** *of how fast and how far they had traveled.*

A ship's captain could use **dead reckoning** to make an **estimate** of how fast the ship was moving. Then, he could **estimate** how far the ship would travel in an hour or a day. He could use a **compass** to know which way he was heading. He could put all this together to make an **estimate** of where he was.

Explorers used many tools to help them navigate.

El Castillo
de San Marcos

The building on the right is a **fort** in St.
Augustine, Florida, where the Spanish **established**
a settlement in 1565. It is the oldest **continuously
occupied** European settlement in the United
States. You can visit there today and still see the old
buildings standing.

This **fort** was built by the Spanish in the 1600s.
It is called El Castillo de San Marcos. That is its
Spanish name. Its English name is the Castle (or
Fort) of Saint Mark.

El Castillo de San Marcos was not the first **fort**
the Spanish built in St. Augustine. The Spanish built
seven or eight **forts** before they built this one. But
these earlier **forts** were made of wood and were not
very strong. Some of them were **destroyed** in wars.
Others were **wrecked** by hurricanes. In 1672, the
Spanish decided to build a new **fort**. This time, they
decided they would use stone to make it strong.

The inside of the **fort** is shaped like a square. On each corner, there is a **bastion** shaped like an arrow. A **bastion** is a raised gun platform. The **bastions** stick out from the **fort**. They let the Spanish fire out of the **fort** in just about any direction.

This is what a **bastion** looks like from the ground.

Imagine you are a soldier. Would you like to attack a **bastion** like this? How would you do it?

If you tried to get close, Spaniards on top of the **bastion** would open fire. They would shoot at you with guns and cannons.

If you got close enough to set up a ladder, the men in the **fort** would tip it over. They might drop hot oil on you. Ouch!

You could try to attack with cannons. But the walls of the **fort** are thick and strong. A few cannonballs would not harm them. But don't forget, the Spanish had cannons of their own. They would fire back at you and you would not have thick stone walls to hide behind!

*A **bastion***

43

Can you guess what the walls of El Castillo de San Marcos are made of? Believe it or not, they are made of seashells! The Spanish used a kind of rock called coquina. Coquina is a mixture of **fossils** and seashells.

Look at the stone on the right. It is coquina. Can you see the seashells? Those shells are the remains of tiny animals that lived in the sea long, long ago.

The Spanish found coquina along the Florida seashore. They used it to build the **fort**.

Coquina turned out to be a good stone for building **forts**. It is softer than other rocks. That means it does not crack or **shatter** when cannonballs hit it. A cannonball might make a dent in a coquina wall or it might be absorbed into the wall. But, in most cases, it would not crack the wall.

Coquina

The **fort** was surrounded by a **moat**. It is no longer filled with water. It is now a dry **moat**.

There was only one way into the **fort**. You had to enter a mini-**fort** that stood just in front of the main **fort**. This mini-**fort** was called the **ravelin**.

A bridge led from the **ravelin** across the **moat** and into the main **fort**. The last part of this bridge was a drawbridge. It could be lifted up to keep people from getting in.

It was not easy to open the drawbridge. It took five men fifteen minutes to open it.

In this image, you can see the bridge that leads into the **fort**. It is on the left.

El Castillo de San Marcos was a strong **fortress**. It was attacked many times but it was never captured.

drawbridge

*The drawbridge leading from the **ravelin** to the main **fort***

6 Coronado Reports to the King

Francisco Vasquez de Coronado was a Spanish conquistador. He explored what is now the American Southwest in search of the Seven Cities of Cibola [SEE-boe-lə], which were said to have streets paved with gold. During the trip, Coronado wrote letters to the King of Spain. In his second letter, written in October of 1541, he described his march across the Great **Plains** to Quivira [Kee-VEE-rə], in modern-day Kansas. He told the king about the native people he and his men met. He also described the buffalo they saw, which he called "cows." On the pages that follow is an edited version of Coronado's letter.

Coronado

Your Majesty,

After I sent my last letter, I met some native people from a **distant** land. They **boasted** of their land, which is called Quivira. They said the men there lived in large houses. They said their chiefs dined on dishes made of gold. I did not know whether to believe these reports. I made up my mind to go and see Quivira.

We set off last spring and reached the **plains**. These **plains** were **vast**—so **vast** that we could not see the end of them. They were flat and open with grasses that blow in the breeze. We traveled over them for more than 300 **leagues**. The **plains** were full of cows. There were too many of them to count. There was not a single day when we did not see some of them.

A buffalo, which Coronado called a "cow"

After 17 days, we met some native people. They are called Querechos [Ker-AE-koez]. They do not plant crops. They travel around with the cows. They eat the flesh of the cows they kill. They **tan** the skins of the cows and make clothes from them. They have little tents made of cowhide. They live in these tents while they travel around with the cows. They have dogs that carry their tents and poles from place to place.

We traveled 42 days more. At times, it was hard to find the way. On the **plains**, there are few landmarks. There are no hills. There are no stones, trees, or shrubs. All we could see was a sea of grass.

We lived on the flesh of the cows we killed. We went many days without water. Sometimes, what we drank was more mud than water. There are no trees on the **plains** except by the rivers. So, we could rarely find firewood.

Tents made of "cowhide"

After 77 days, we arrived in Quivira.

This was the place our guides had described. They had told us of stone houses that were many stories tall. But we found only little grass huts. There were only a few people in the place and they were as **barbarous** as the others we have met. They swore to obey Your Majesty and placed themselves under your **royal lordship**.

The natives gave me a piece of **copper**. I have sent this back to the **viceroy** of New Spain. I have not seen any other metal in these parts except this and some little **copper** bells.

We stayed in Quivira for 25 days. I searched the nearby lands to see if there is anything which could be of service to Your Majesty. Besides the land itself and people who live on it, I have not found or heard of anything. I am sure there is no gold here.

Copper

The land in Quivira is the best I have seen for producing crops. The soil is black. The land is well-watered by springs and rivers. I found some **prunes** like those in Spain. There are some nuts. There are also very good sweet grapes and **mulberries**.

I have treated the natives as well as was possible, as Your Majesty commanded. They have received no harm in any way from me or from those who went in my company.

This is my report. I have done all that I possibly could to serve Your Majesty. I remain Your Majesty's **humble** servant and **vassal**,

Francisco Vasquez de Coronado

*The **plains** with buffalo, called "cows" by Coronado*

John Cabot

Chapter

7

John Cabot (known as Giovanni Caboto [JEE-oe-VO-nee CA-bu-toe] in his native Italy) had the same dream as Columbus: to reach Asia by sailing west. However, unlike Columbus, Cabot thought the best chance of reaching Asia would be to sail around the northern part of Earth, where the distance around would be **substantially** shorter than the distance at the **equator**. Cabot, like other explorers, wanted to find the Northwest Passage, which was thought to be a shorter route west from Europe to Asia. Finding a shorter route to Asia meant finding a shorter route to spices.

Many details of Cabot's life and voyages are unknown. He did not keep records during his voyages nor was much written about his life. However, it is known that he was Italian and had support from King Henry VII of England for his voyages. King Henry VII gave Cabot a **charter** to explore and **claim** land for England.

John Cabot

Cabot made his first **attempt** to find the Northwest Passage in 1496. This **attempt** was a failure. He had a disagreement with some members of his crew. There was also a **shortage** of food and he ran into bad weather. Cabot decided to turn back for England.

Cabot tried again in 1497, with a single ship and a crew of 18. This time, he reached land, which he thought was Asia. However, this land turned out to be the coast of North America. It is not known exactly where he first sighted land, though. It may have been the coast of Newfoundland. Cabot spent a short time exploring the coast and it is possible that he sailed as far south as the Chesapeake Bay. During this voyage, Cabot found a large area of **shallow** water that was abundant with fish. This area, known as the Grand Banks, is still one of the best fishing areas in the world today. At any rate, Cabot and his men became one of the first European **expeditions** to see the **landmass** now known as North America.

The circled area is the Grand Banks.

Cabot sailed back to England with his news. Certain that he had found a new, shorter route to Asia, Cabot gained support for another, much larger **expedition**. This **expedition** left England in 1498, but it never returned. Nobody knows for certain what happened to Cabot and his men. In time, it became clear that Cabot had not, in fact, located the Northwest Passage. However, England based its later **claims** to North American **territory** on Cabot's explorations. When Cabot had first sighted land, he had gone **ashore** and **claimed** it for England. Cabot's exploration began England's desire to explore and create settlements in North America.

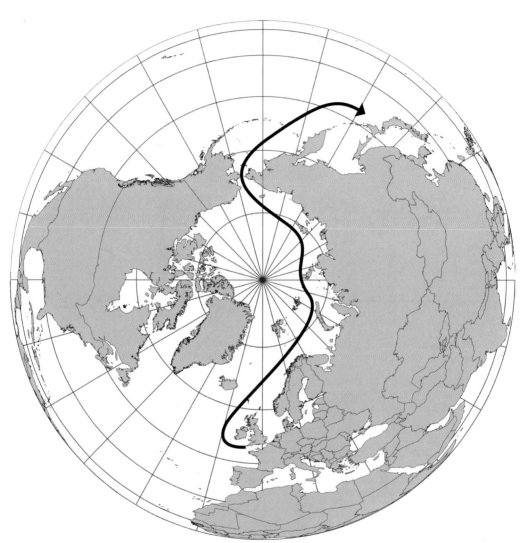

The route Cabot intended to take to find the Northwest Passage

Do you think you could be a sailor on Cabot's ship? Here is a description of what it might be like to be a young sailor.

On a ship, young boys served as **pages**. On land, a **page** worked for a knight. At sea, he worked for a captain. **Pages** did all sorts of odd jobs. They carried messages, mopped the deck, helped pass out food, and cleaned up after meals.

Older boys might be asked to work the **bilge pumps**. Even the best ships sometimes sprang a leak. If a ship leaked too much, it might sink. To keep that from happening, sailors had to pump water out of the ship using a **bilge pump**. This was a terrible job. The bilge water was disgusting. It smelled bad and it made the sailors sick.

After pumping bilge water all day, it would have been great to sit down to a nice, warm meal. Unfortunately, sailors did not get many warm meals. For most meals, they got **hardtack**.

A bilge pump used in Cabot's time

Hardtack was a kind of bread that was baked over and over. **Hardtack** was so hard, it was tough to eat. Sailors had to soak it in a drink to soften it up. The good thing about **hardtack**, though, was that it would not **spoil** on a long voyage. It was so hard, bugs had trouble getting into it—unless it got wet. Once it got wet, **weevils** and other bugs could and did get into it. But you could usually see them and brush them off with your fingers.

If a voyage was going well, sailors might get other kinds of food. They might get a little salted meat now and then. They might get some fish or a few beans. But if supplies were running low, they might get nothing but **hardtack**.

The diet on sailing ships was so bad that many sailors got sick. Lots of them got a disease called **scurvy**. Today, we know now that **scurvy** is caused by a lack of vitamin C, found in fresh fruits and vegetables. In the Age of Exploration, people did not know this. So many sailors died.

Hardtack

After a long day of work, sailors were ready to fall into bed and rest their aching bones. They were ready—but there were no beds for them to fall into. The captain had a bed to sleep in, but the sailors did not. They slept on the deck. As the ship rolled back and forth with the waves, the sailors rolled with it.

Most sailors had to stand **watch** for part of the night. When that was done, they could sleep for a few hours. In the morning, they would get up and do it all over again. A sailor's day started bright and early.

So, what do you think? Does a sailor's life sound good to you?

*Sailors stood **watch** on the platform high up on the mast.*

Henry Hudson

An Englishman named Henry Hudson tried four times to find the Northwest Passage. He died trying.

First, in 1607, he tried sailing north from England. If you look at a globe, you can see what he was trying to do. He understood that Earth was round and he thought he could sail across the North Pole. He didn't understand that **solid** ice always covers the Arctic Ocean. "I hoped to have a clear sea," Hudson wrote of his first journey, but "that proved impossible due to the ice surrounding us."

Hudson tried again in 1608. He sailed northeast and again found **icebergs** and freezing weather. He turned his boat around and tried sailing northwest. When his crew realized that they weren't heading home, they **rebelled** against Hudson, saying they wouldn't work unless they sailed to England. So, home they went.

*Hudson encountered **icebergs** and freezing weather.*

In 1609, Henry Hudson sailed west. This time, he was working for a group of businessmen called the Dutch East India Company. On this trip, he reached North America and claimed land for Holland.

Hudson saw many native people. One man who sailed with him wrote in his journal, "They are well-dressed in loose deer skins and brought green tobacco which they gave us in exchange for knives and beads." The native people also gave the sailors bread made of **maize**.

Hudson sailed past "a very good piece of ground and a cliff close by of white-green color...on the side of the river called Manna-hata." It was the island we now call Manhattan (the center of New York City today). Next, Hudson sailed up a river that still bears his name. You'll find the Hudson River on a map of the state of New York.

Manhattan is the center of New York City today.

In 1610, Hudson tried once more to find a shortcut from Europe to Asia. He sailed a ship called *Discovery* into a wide **expanse** of water in the northern part of Canada. Today, it is named after him: the Hudson Bay.

On the map, the Hudson Bay looks like a big, open body of water. But in many places, the water gets too shallow for sailing. In many other places, it is frozen **solid** almost all year long. Once again, Henry Hudson had sailed into icy waters, just as winter was coming.

Hudson and his crew went ashore during the winter. They ran short of food and water. Some of the crew got sick. Some died. The sailors blamed Hudson for caring more about finding the Northwest Passage than about keeping his crew safe and healthy.

When the ice began to melt, the crew **rebelled**. They forced Hudson, his son, and a few crew members loyal to Hudson to get into a small boat with no oars. Then, they left them behind and sailed the *Discovery* back to England. No one ever heard from Henry Hudson again.

Hudson and others were left in a boat with no oars.

The Fur Trade and Samuel de Champlain

Many of the Frenchmen who came to North America in the 1600s and 1700s were fur **traders**. These **traders traded** with the native people. They gave them European goods **in exchange** for animal skins and furs.

The **traders** collected many kinds of fur but they were most interested in beaver **pelts**. Beaver hats were popular in Europe. You could sell beaver hats in England, France, Germany, and Russia.

Why were beaver hats so popular? For one thing, beaver fur is thick. It is thick enough to keep your head warm in a cold Russian winter and it is waterproof. Rain runs off a beaver hat. Your head stays dry.

Some hat makers used the beaver fur as it was. They made soft, puffy hats. Others processed the beaver fur to make **felt**. The smooth, waterproof **felt** was then formed into hats. **Felt** hats did not look like they were made of beaver fur. But, they were.

A beaver hat

In many parts of Europe, there were no beavers left. Hunters had killed too many of them. The beaver had almost gone extinct. Europeans could not get beaver **pelts** at home. So, they were willing to pay for beaver **pelts** imported from North America.

Samuel de Champlain and other Frenchmen took the lead in the fur **trade**. They set up **trading posts** in North America. There were **trading posts** along the Atlantic Coast. There were **trading posts** in Quebec and along the St. Lawrence River. There were even **trading posts** farther west, along the shores of the Great Lakes.

On the page that follows is an adaptation of Champlain's journey down the River of the Iroquois to the lake that came to bear his name: Lake Champlain.

*A **trading post***

July, 1609

We continued on our journey until we came to an island. The island was about three leagues long and had the **finest** pine trees that I had ever seen. We went hunting here and captured some wild animals.

The next day, we started out again, floating down the river as far as the entrance to a large lake. There were many pretty islands there. They all contained many **fine** forests and **lush** meadows. There were too many birds to count. Also, we saw all kinds of wild animals such as deer with their young fawns, bears, and many animals that move from the mainland over to the islands and back again. We captured many of these animals as well. There were many rivers that emptied into the lake as well as dense forests of **fine** trees. I found chestnut trees on the border of the lake. I had never seen trees like this before. There were great numbers of fish in the lake.

I noticed that many of the mountains in the distance to the north had snow on top of them. I was told that the Iroquois lived there and that there were many beautiful valleys with fruit and grain there.

Lake Champlain in the fall

Many different native groups lived in these lands. The French made **treaties** with some of them, including the Algonquin [al-GON-kwin] people and the Huron [HYER-on] people. The French agreed to **trade** with these people and not fight with them.

The native people would bring beaver **pelts** to **trade**. In some cases, they would bring **pelts** they had gathered themselves. In other cases, they would bring **pelts** they had **obtained** by **trading** with other native people.

The French would **barter** with the native people. They would give the native people things they wanted **in exchange** for the beaver **pelts**.

A beaver has thick fur that was used to make hats.

Many of the things the native people wanted were made of metal. Most native people did not make their own metal products. They had to **trade** for these items. Many native people **traded** furs for knives and ax blades. Others **traded** for kettles and fish hooks. Still others **traded** for glass beads from Europe, which were highly desirable.

The French would gather up lots of beaver **pelts**. Then, they would ship the **pelts** back to France and sell them. They made a lot of money doing this, so they did it again and again.

As time went on, the French learned what the native people liked. They learned that many native people would **trade** beaver **pelts** for wool blankets. Some would **trade** for tobacco. Others would **trade** for guns and gunpowder.

The Age of Exploration

*Items like tobacco, kettles, and fish hooks were **traded** for **pelts**.*

In 2011, the people of Canada put an image of a beaver on the back of their nickel. They did not put the beaver on their nickel because he is cute. They put the beaver there because the fur **trade** is an important part of the history of Canada. For two hundred years, the fur **trade** was a source of **income** for the French and the native people alike.

A beaver

A History of People in North America

Lots of people think that Columbus was the first to arrive in America. But that's not right. There are at least two other groups of people who settled in North America and both of them got there many years before Christopher Columbus.

Map of North America

One group was the Vikings.

The Vikings lived in Northern Europe, in Scandinavia. They sailed around a lot, **raiding** and robbing as they went. The image on the next page shows you some of the places they explored and some of the Vikings who were explorers.

In 982, some Vikings left Iceland and settled in Greenland, which is part of North America. They arrived there about 500 years before Columbus sailed. The Viking settlements on Greenland grew for a while. Archaeologists estimate there were probably 3,000 to 5,000 Viking settlers there at one point. Eventually, however, the Vikings left. Viking settlements in Greenland seem to have been **abandoned** in the 1400s, not long before the voyage of Columbus.

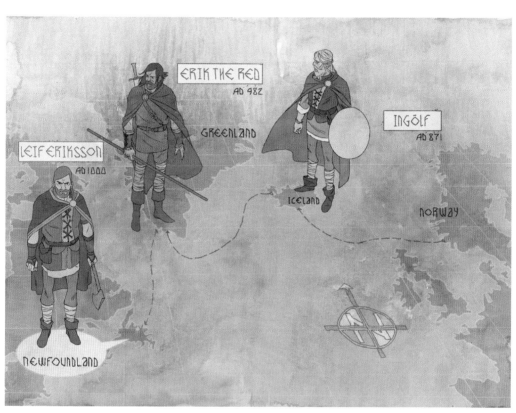

This image shows some of the places the Vikings explored and some of the Vikings who explored.

The Vikings also explored lands west of Greenland. Around the year 1000, the famous Viking explorer Leif Eriksson visited a land he and other Vikings called Vinland. Most experts believe Vinland was somewhere along the coast of Newfoundland, in modern-day Canada. There is **evidence** that some Vikings settled in Newfoundland. In 1960, the ruins of a Viking village were found there. This village may have been part of Vinland.

The Vikings definitely got to America before Columbus. So maybe we should say the Vikings were the first Europeans to settle in North America. But before we decide, we need to look at another group that settled in North America.

The Age of Exploration

A reconstructed Viking structure at L'Anse aux Meadows in Canada

Another group to settle in North America was the Native Americans.

Although we call these people "Native" Americans, they did not always live in the Americas. They came to America from Asia. When and how this happened are subjects of much debate.

Some historians think the first settlers made their way to North America a little more than 15,000 years ago. Others think the first people came to America many years earlier—perhaps even 40,000 years ago. Some experts think these people came by land, at a time when Alaska and Asia were connected by land. Others think they may have traveled along the coast in boats.

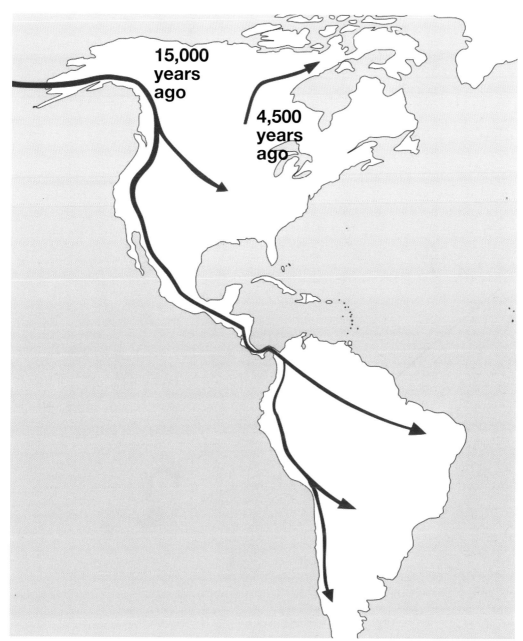

When the first settlers came to North America is a subject of much debate.

The map on the next page shows how we think human beings spread around the earth. Experts think the first humans lived in Africa. About 100,000 years ago, some humans moved out of Africa and into the Middle East. About 70,000 years ago, a group of humans moved into southeast Asia. About 15,000 years ago—or possibly earlier—some of these people crossed from Asia to the Americas. It is believed that many people also came to North America by various ship routes.

New archeological discoveries continue to be made every day about early settlers in North America. These discoveries change our understanding of who lived in North America in the past.

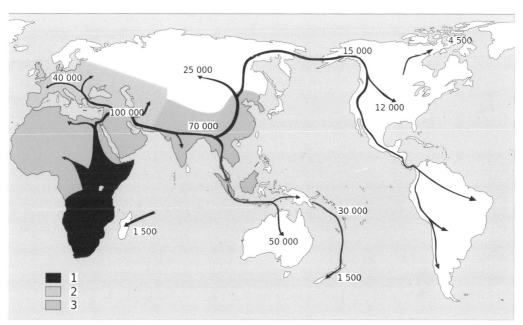

This map shows how people today think human beings spread around the earth. The numbers represent "years ago."

11 Caribbean Words

Did you know that some words we use every day come from the Caribbean, an area of islands between North and South America? These are words that were used by native people before Columbus and the conquistadors came. Later, they were picked up by Europeans who came to the New World, including English speakers.

For each of the following words, there are clues that will help you try to guess it.

The area inside the gray line on the map is part of the Caribbean.

Clues for Word #1

- This word describes a big storm.

- The winds in this storm swirl around in a big circle. This kind of storm is sort of like a tornado but it's much bigger. However, unlike a tornado, this kind of storm usually travels over water. It gets weaker when it travels over land.

- People who live on the east coast of the U.S. have to worry about this kind of storm. The winds it brings can damage houses near the beach and can even knock houses to the ground.

- The name of this storm sort of rhymes with window pane.

What is the word? (Turn the page to see the answer.)

A tornado

Answer to last riddle: *hurricane*

The word, hurricane, comes from the Carib language. The people of the Caribbean know all about hurricanes because several of these big storms sweep through the Caribbean every year. Most of the storms occur in the summer and the fall.

Clues for Word #2

- This word is a kind of boat.

- This is a small boat that seats two or three people.

- The people in the boat face forward and use paddles to make it go. The person in front usually pulls straight back using a paddle. The person in back uses a paddle to **steer**.

- It's best not to stand up in this kind of boat. If you do, it might tip over.

- This word sort of rhymes with bamboo.

The effects of a hurricane

Answer to last riddle: *canoe*

The people of the Caribbean used canoes to paddle from island to island. They cut down a tree. Using tools and fire, they dug out a canoe from the tree trunk. People in other places also used this kind of boat. But the word, canoe, comes from the Caribbean.

Clues for Word #3

- This word names a kind of food and also a kind of cooking.

- If your dad cooks outside over a smoky fire, he probably likes this kind of cooking.

- Some people like to cook pork this way. Other people like to cook beef or chicken.

- Another way to say this word is BBQ.

A dugout canoe

Answer to last riddle: *barbecue*

The people of the Caribbean cooked food over an open fire and called it barbricot. This is where the word, barbecue, sometimes spelled as barbeque, came from.

Clues for Word #4

- This is a vegetable that was unknown in Europe before the Spanish arrived in the New World, but then it quickly spread around the world.

- Some people like to eat this vegetable baked. They might put butter on top or maybe sour cream.

- Other people like to thinly slice this vegetable and cook it in hot oil. This makes chips that crunch in your mouth.

- Still other people like to cut this vegetable into long, skinny rectangles and fry it. If you've ever had french fries, you have tasted this vegetable.

Barbecue cooking on a grill

Answer to last riddle: *potato*

The potato is a New World crop. This root vegetable was grown in what is now Peru, in South America. It was also grown elsewhere in the Americas. The people of Peru called it the papa. The Caribbean people called it the batata. The Spanish called it the patata. We call it the potato.

The potato was eventually carried back to Europe. People discovered that it was **cheap** and grew well in many countries. By the late 1700s, lots of farmers in Europe were growing potatoes. The potato became an important crop.

French fries seem to have been invented a little later, probably in France. Thomas Jefferson mentioned fried potatoes around 1805, probably learning about them from a French cook.

Today, french fries are very **popular**. You can order them in tons of restaurants all around the world.

Potatoes and french fries

Glossary for
The Age of Exploration

A

abandon—to leave somewhere, never to return (**abandoned**)

accurate—correct

ashore—on land

attempt—an act of trying

B

barbarous—wild, sometimes violent

barter—to trade by exchanging goods and services instead of paying or accepting money for them

bastion—a raised gun platform in a fort

bilge pump—a device used to remove water from the bottom part of a ship

boast—to brag (**boasted**)

C

charter—a formal document that gives rights to a person or group of people; Kings often issued charters to explorers so explorers would search for land and treasure on behalf of the king.

cheap—does not cost much

claim—to say something belongs to you (**claims, claimed**)

compass—a tool used for finding directions with a magnetic pointer that always points north

conquistador—a former warrior, usually from Spain, who took control of something by force (**conquistadors**)

continuously—without stopping

convince—to talk someone into something by giving good reasons (**convinced**)

copper—a reddish-brown mineral found in the earth

D

dead reckoning—a way to measure speed when traveling through water by throwing a knotted rope with a piece of wood on the end overboard and observing how much of and how fast the rope is pulled into the water

destroy—to completely ruin so that it no longer exists (**destroyed**)

device—a piece of equipment that does a specific job

distant—far away

E

equator—an imaginary line around the middle of the earth that is equally far from both the North Pole and South Pole

establish—to start something that is meant to last a long time (**established**)

estate—everything a person owns

estimate—(verb) to make a guess based on information you have; (noun) a guess made based on information you have

evidence—information that helps show if something is either true or not true

expanse—a large, open area

expect—to think something will probably happen (**expected**)

expedition—a long trip made for a specific purpose (**expeditions**)

expensive—costs a lot of money

explorer—a person who sets out to find new things (**exploration**, **explorations**, **explorers**, **explored**, **exploring**)

F

felt—thick cloth made from wool, fur, or other fibers

fine—excellent (**finest**)

flavor—taste (**flavors**)

forerunner—something that came before

fort—a large building constructed to survive enemy attacks

fortress—a strong fort

fossil—a bone, shell, or other remains of a plant or animal from millions of years ago that has formed rock (**fossils**)

funding—money provided for a special purpose

G

gadget—a small tool (**gadgets**)

grind—to crush something into small pieces or powder (**ground**)

H

hardtack—hard bread that has been baked many times

hourglass—a tool for measuring time; It is a glass container with an upper part and lower part connected in the middle by a narrow tube and sand falls from the upper part into the lower part in a fixed amount of time, usually an hour.

hull—the outer covering of a seed or fruit

humble—respectful, not thinking you are better than others

I

iceberg—a large mass of ice floating in the ocean (**icebergs**)

import—to bring in from somewhere else (**imported**)

impressive—deserving attention or respect

in exchange—the act of giving something and receiving something of similar value in return

income—money earned, mostly from working

inherit—to receive money, property, and other things when someone dies (**inherits**, **inherited**)

K

keep track—to continue to be aware of (**keeping track**, **kept track**)

kernel—seed

L

landmark—an object on land that is easy to see and recognize (**landmarks**)

landmass—a large, continuous area of land, such as a continent

league—a distance between 2.4 and 4.6 miles

lordship—authority and power of a lord or high-ranking person

lush—covered with healthy, green plants

M

magnet—a piece of metal that attracts iron or steel and has a north and south pole; Earth is a magnet. (**magnets**)

magnetic field—the area around each pole of a magnet that has the power to attract other metals

maize—corn

method—a way of doing things

moat—a deep ditch, usually filled with water, dug around a fort or castle to prevent enemy attacks

mulberry—a dark purple berry (**mulberries**)

N

noble—a person from a family of high social rank, similar to patricians in ancient Rome (**nobles**)

O

obtain—to get (**obtained**)

occupied—lived and worked in

overrun—to exist in large numbers

overwhelm—to take over completely

P

page—a boy servant (**pages**)

pelt—an animal skin with fur still on it (**pelts**)

peppercorn—a dried berry from a plant that is used to make pepper (**peppercorns**)

plain—a large, flat area of land with no trees (**plains**)

popular—liked by many people

precious—very valuable

property—buildings, land, and livestock that someone owns

prune—a dried plum (**prunes**)

R

raid—to attack by surprise (**raiding**)

ravelin—a small building you must pass through first in order to enter a fort or castle

rebel—to fight against the person or people in charge (**rebelled**)

royal—relating to a king or queen

S

scarce—hard to find

scroll—a paper rolled up into a tube (**scrolls**)

scurvy—a disease caused by not eating enough fruits or vegetables with vitamin C, leading to spongy gums, loose teeth, skin spots, and sometimes death

shallow—not deep

shatter—to suddenly break into many small pieces

shortage—when there is not enough

slash—to make a path by cutting plants (**slashed**)

solid—firm and hard

spice—a substance from a plant that has a specific smell or taste and is used to add flavor to food (**spices**)

spoil—to become rotten and not able to be eaten

steer—to control the direction of

substantially—great in size, value, or importance

T

tan—to turn animal skin into leather using a specific process

territory—a large area of land with defined boundaries

throne—the power and authority of a king or queen

trade—(verb) to exchange something you have for something someone else has; (noun) the act of exchanging goods (**traders**, **traded**, **trading**)

trading post—a place far away from towns where people buy, sell, and trade things (**trading posts**)

treaty—a formal agreement between groups of people, often to stop fighting (**treaties**)

V

vassal—a person who is loyal and serves a lord or king

vast—very great in size or amount

viceroy—a person sent by the king to rule a colony

voyage—a long journey, usually by water

W

watch—the time that someone is on duty to guard or protect something

weevil—a small beetle (**weevils**)

whiz—a person who is extremely skilled at something

wreck—to destroy, ruin (**wrecked**)

CORE KNOWLEDGE LANGUAGE ARTS

SERIES EDITOR-IN-CHIEF
E. D. Hirsch, Jr.

PRESIDENT
Linda Bevilacqua

EDITORIAL STAFF
Carolyn Gosse, Senior Editor - Preschool
Khara Turnbull, Materials Development Manager
Michelle L. Warner, Senior Editor - Listening & Learning

Mick Anderson
Robin Blackshire
Maggie Buchanan
Paula Coyner
Sue Fulton
Sara Hunt
Erin Kist
Robin Luecke
Rosie McCormick
Cynthia Peng
Liz Pettit
Ellen Sadler
Deborah Samley
Diane Auger Smith
Sarah Zelinke

DESIGN AND GRAPHICS STAFF
Scott Ritchie, Creative Director

Kim Berrall
Michael Donegan
Liza Greene
Matt Leech
Bridget Moriarty
Lauren Pack

CONSULTING PROJECT MANAGEMENT SERVICES
ScribeConcepts.com

ADDITIONAL CONSULTING SERVICES
Ang Blanchette
Dorrit Green
Carolyn Pinkerton

ACKNOWLEDGMENTS
These materials are the result of the work, advice, and encouragement of numerous individuals over many years. Some of those singled out here already know the depth of our gratitude; others may be surprised to find themselves thanked publicly for help they gave quietly and generously for the sake of the enterprise alone. To helpers named and unnamed we are deeply grateful.

CONTRIBUTORS TO EARLIER VERSIONS OF THESE MATERIALS
Susan B. Albaugh, Kazuko Ashizawa, Nancy Braier, Kathryn M. Cummings, Michelle De Groot, Diana Espinal, Mary E. Forbes, Michael L. Ford, Ted Hirsch, Danielle Knecht, James K. Lee, Diane Henry Leipzig, Martha G. Mack, Liana Mahoney, Isabel McLean, Steve Morrison, Juliane K. Munson, Elizabeth B. Rasmussen, Laura Tortorelli, Rachael L. Shaw, Sivan B. Sherman, Miriam E. Vidaver, Catherine S. Whittington, Jeannette A. Williams

We would like to extend special recognition to Program Directors Matthew Davis and Souzanne Wright who were instrumental to the early development of this program.

SCHOOLS
We are truly grateful to the teachers, students, and administrators of the following schools for their willingness to field test these materials and for their invaluable advice: Capitol View Elementary, Challenge Foundation Academy (IN), Community Academy Public Charter School, Lake Lure Classical Academy, Lepanto Elementary School, New Holland Core Knowledge Academy, Paramount School of Excellence, Pioneer Challenge Foundation Academy, New York City PS 26R (The Carteret School), PS 30X (Wilton School), PS 50X (Clara Barton School), PS 96Q, PS 102X (Joseph O. Loretan), PS 104Q (The Bays Water), PS 214K (Michael Friedsam), PS 223Q (Lyndon B. Johnson School), PS 308K (Clara Cardwell), PS 333Q (Goldie Maple Academy), Sequoyah Elementary School, South Shore Charter Public School, Spartanburg Charter School, Steed Elementary School, Thomas Jefferson Classical Academy, Three Oaks Elementary, West Manor Elementary.

And a special thanks to the CKLA Pilot Coordinators Anita Henderson, Yasmin Lugo-Hernandez, and Susan Smith, whose suggestions and day-to-day support to teachers using these materials in their classrooms was critical.

CREDITS

EXPERT REVIEWER
J. Chris Arndt, Jeffrey L. Hantman

WRITERS
Matt Davis

ILLUSTRATORS AND IMAGE SOURCES
Cover: Spirit of America / Shutterstock.com; Title Page: Spirit of America / Shutterstock.com; 5: Spirit of Smerica / Shutterstock.com; 7: Library of Congress, Prints & Photographs Division, LC-DIG-pga-02388; 9 (Columbus): Library of Congress, Prints & Photographs Division, LC-DIG-pga-02388; 9 (Coronado): Angela Padron; 9 (Cabot): public domain; 9 (Hudson): public domain; 9 (Champlain): public domain; 11: Shutterstock; 13: Shutterstock; 15: Shutterstock; 17: Shutterstock; 19: Shutterstock; 21: Core Knowledge Staff; 23: Core Knowledge Staff; 25: Spirit of America / Shutterstock.com; 27: public domain; 29: public domain; 31: public domain; 33: public domain; 35: Shutterstock; 37: Shutterstock; 39 (top): Shutterstock; 39 (bottom): Sage Ross / Wikimedia Commons / Creative Commons Attribution-Share Alike 2.0 Generic, http://creativecommons.org/licenses/by-sa/2.0/deed.en / Modified from Original; 41: Shutterstock; 43: Shutterstock; 45: Shutterstock; 47: Shutterstock; 49: Shutterstock; 51: Shutterstock; 53: Angela Padron; 55: Shutterstock; 57: Shutterstock; 59: Shutterstock; 61: Shutterstock; 63: public domain; 65: Shutterstock; 67: Shutterstock; 69: Core Knowledge Staff; 71: DryPot / Wikimedia Commons / Creative Commons Attribution 2.5 Generic, http://creativecommons.org/licenses/by/2.5/deed.en / Modified from Original; 73: Shutterstock; 75: Shutterstock; 77: Shutterstock; 79: public domain; 81: Shutterstock; 83: Shutterstock; 85: Shutterstock; 87: Shutterstock; 89: Shutterstock; 91: Shutterstock; 93: Shutterstock; 95: Jacob Wyatt; 97: Shutterstock; 99: Shutterstock; 101: Shutterstock; 103: Shutterstock; 105: Shutterstock; 107: Shutterstock; 109: Shutterstock; 111: Shutterstock; 113: Shutterstock